Fighting Fermi

By

Andrew Najberg

Fighting Fermi

By

Andrew Najberg

WALNUT STREET
PUBLISHING

ISBN: 979-8-9909790-5-5

Walnut Street Publishing
1673 S Holtzclaw Ave
Chattanooga, TN 37404

TABLE OF CONTENTS

Part V – The Ninth Filter

Acknowledgements

"Anthill by the Mailbox Post" originally appeared in *The Bangalore Review*, April 2019

"Composition of the Planets" originally appeared in *Plato's Cave Online*, October 2022

"Fighting Fermi" originally appeared through Brain Mills Press, May 2022, and won their 2022 National Poetry Month contest.

"Glory of Now" originally appeared in *HASH Journal,* January 2021

"How I believe in ghosts" appeared in *North American Review* June 2022

"How to Carry On" appeared in *Good River Review* April 2022

"How We Keep Tending" forthcoming in *Canary Literary Magazine* Late 2023

"Natural Embrace" appeared in *In Parentheses* Vol 6 Issue 3 Winter 2021

"Parenting" originally appeared in *Faultline Journal* Spring 2019

"Pick their grief like berries" forthcoming in *Last Stanza* Summer 2023

"Saturn Garden" originally appeared in *Plato's Cave Online*, October 2022

"Scrying" forthcoming in *Illumen* Fall 2023

"Soul brawl" appeared in *Stoneboat Literary Journal*, Issue 11 Volume 1 Spring 2021.

"The Ladybug" appeared in *Symposeum* issue 5, Winter 2023

"There is always one left" appeared in *Asheville Poetry Review* Spring 2022

"Things You Need to Know" appeared in *Symposeum* issue 3, Fall 2021

"Things You Don't Need to Know" appeared in *In Parenthesis* Vol 6 Issue 3 Winter 2021

"Those from Ryugu" forthcoming in *Illumen* Fall 2023

"When I grow up" appeared in *Coastal Shelf* End-of-Year 2021 Issue

"When the path forks ahead" in *Ghost City Review*, April 2023.

"Why we don't want the gates open" appeared in *Mockingheart Review*, February 2020

"Year of the Rat" appeared in *Broad River Review* Fall 2021

"Yesterday, the split of prokaryotes" appeared in *Coastal Shelf* Fall 2021

PART I

ASTIGMAT

How to Carry On

Hard to avoid poisons
    in soil and shelved
        in sealed boxes.
They say the earth,
    the water,
        sooner or later the stars.

Even blowing kisses adds carbon.

We can't wear our own skin
    without worry, shouldn't be allowed
      to allow ourselves
      genuine human affection.

At the park, I walk my daughter under kite
    strings and past drone pilots.
    A grandfather with charcoal bricks
      at his heel presses burgers
      against a grill.

My girl kneels in the grass
    and bites the head off a dandelion.
      Look daddy, I'm a horse,
      she sputters, already in search
      of another. I rest my hand
on her shoulder,

    pull her nose from clover.

Of course you are.

We talk about things that only matter

in that we're talking, run
      around each other on the incline
      until the sun falls low over the trees.

It grows cool
      as parents pack their kids into car seats.

The swings ease still on their chains.
      The metal slides,
            crickets land on their rails.

Is it nighttime?
      And I want to say not yet,
            that the dark isn't total,

but light dims behind mountains
      and no moon has risen
            to lead the way.

Night Blooms

The first day   I led you out
the front door   and down those
                                                                steps

to the broken walk
            past drainage   trench litter   and rusted

                    tracks
                        with split ties and

into that-

World

            You will succeed   at failing,
                    I told myself,   get it wrong,
                                                    but get it at
                                            all.

You found a flower you felt meant to pick
            sprouted from a rust-hole   in a chain-link post,

        and then   at dusk

        the things wrong with my eyes
                                            cast radiant blossoms
        from   every   streetlight.

Though you couldn't see them as I carried you,   they were

                                                    there
                                        for you.

The Glory of Now

In one eye, headlines like "Florida Man
Arrested for Practicing Karate on Swans,"
and, in the other, an old student
with whom I haven't spoken for years
fears an old, mutual acquaintance
I'd forgotten is a suicide risk.

On the TV, a bad remake of a bad movie.
In the middle, the screen this poem inhabits.
None of them know how often I minimize the others.
Meanwhile, everywhere someone seems unaware
they're abusing something. I'm unsure of my crime
but no doubt I must be committing one.

Everything untainted has been measured into glasses
and used to play a symphony with silverware.
There is a video on YouTube. It plays after
central African violence but before
the information paradox. Then, three clips
of cats that failed to become viral.

It's okay though. We can help each other remotely
in ways never before imagined. White masks
on elastic bands and non-latex hypoallergenic gloves
become wholly unnecessary once we abstract
human assistance. After all, binary is of one and not one.
We don't even need to make eye contact.

Your hand makes the same motion to enact compassion
as it does to access click bait and pornography, all

now expressions of instant gratification to elate
ourselves. We can console a thousand in spirit
rather than one we sought out, a relationship
now optional. Take comfort though;

somewhere, there still remains someone without
a screen to bellow through. They don't know
wires or signals or contact. Maybe they live
in a place where dust coats the cookware,
one must hike to wait in a line for water
and you never stop hearing the buzz of insects.

Maybe they brew teas from local flowers,
spend their evenings mending jackets
with different sized needle between
humming, pursed lips, and they rock
on a creaking porch envisioning better
fences and the fortunes they will bring.

I'm letting myself get carried away, I know,
as I pour a coffee, search for clean spoons
and a conscience just dirty enough to be human.
I can't say for sure I've helped myself lately
or that I've lived more than yesterday's script,
but, right now, the kids and my wife sleep.

I check on them and their night lights and find that
blankets rise and fall here and anywhere I look
from the windows. Down at the bottom of the hill
lived the woman who tried to run her family over
with her SUV over some trivial domestic squabble
before she barricaded the home against the police.

I thought I saw sugar in the cabinet the other day.
Now, now I am uncertain, and there is no doubt
that the glue traps in the basement are full.
The movie hasn't stopped. New headlines are in.
No one has died nor are they the wiser. Already,
on the counter, my forgotten drink, somehow,

                                  my thirst too.

Saturn garden

This will be cabbage, I tell him, *tomatoes,*
and kale. Last year, radishes and broccoli.
One too bitter, one went to flower.
Next year, we'll try carrots and potatoes.
He studies the rows and the little wooden
skewers that mark the row, lets a snail
onto his palm, sets it on a grass blade.

Last night, he said he wants there to be turtles
on Saturn, and I tell him that we might land
people on Mars, but I don't think it's quite
the same. I want him to feel comfort
with his hands in the soil and that he might
plant a crop on another planet, perhaps
in some hydroponic pre-fab dome where
you never forget that all you have of home

is what you bring in heart and lungs. I open
the seeds and let him sprinkle them into holes
he bore with thumbs among worms. He stops
to extract a long one longer than his hand
when it uncurls like a broke rubber band on his palm.
One day, perhaps we'll share skies different
in ways no one in history can claim. For now,
I pass him the little spade. Show him
to cover the holes by spreading the dirt.

Year of the Rat

Among the derailed train, a woman wobbles upright,
her shoulder attached only by skin and sinew.

She attempts to sling her purse as if about to enter Macy's
but misses her body altogether.

The handbag crashes to smoking dirt, a red lipstick,
a notepad with a pastel cover tumble to the ground.

Her lungs deflate. She lets out a gentle 'oh',
thinks her nearly severed arm should lift.

It doesn't, so she drops to one knee, then thumps
on her ass, visibly draining from herself.

Among the drive shafts and busted furnace
pokes a rat from a burrow under some rocks.

Its whiskers vibrate as it sniffs oil spray on grass
and things thrown from the dining car.

The secret to immortality is to seek the end of life
and fail to arrive, but the rat doesn't know

the magnitude of the failure around it,
that the wreck of mangled limbs

inside broken berth windows is its windfall.
Carrion birds alight on branches.

Mongrels skirt the scene's edge and
suss which scents appetize.

Eventually, sirens will come, but for now,
computerized watches digitize hearts ceasing.

They are now stored in the cloud,
the rat among their treasures.

A dead man in a blue suit receives
text messages in his pocket

from his daughter driving home from college.
Apparently, traffic has hit a dead standstill,

and she will be more than a little late.
She's going to pick up dinner on the road,

but please, stay up. I have
something important to talk about.

Those from Ryugu

My daughter and I watched the Ryugu probe land
with chute and smoke. Humans learned from religion
to work through avatars: gods never stick fingers in soil.

I wanted to tell her that one day we will travel
to distant planets, but she yawned,
asked if we could fly to the sun. I confessed:

stars aren't things we land on, and I don't really know
what is. Every god wants to be the kind that creates
but I think they only thing we'll ever make are

seeds without soil. Mother Nature doesn't make
promises the way we lie to our children. They'll
always find water to drink. That they can trust

in us to protect them. Natural states leave
parched throats and cracked lips, and my daughter
fluttered her lids, rolled into dreams

strong enough to fuel a rocket. She lay lit by
her constellation nightlight, while I hoped records highs
break like summer clay when the shadows pass.

Almost solitude

Both kids down for a nap
      but I'm not quite alone
as I sit in sun
      on the back stoop.

The monitor mutters
      gravel throat static
      laced with rustling sheets
          to noise machine
          waves

Every sound might be the sound
to which I must react
      or I might hear the wrong silence

My eyes stray
      to the unwatered irises

      to the raspberry patch
         run wild

      to the fence gate's broken latch

So often I feel that an extra
      step to the left
         is the math of ruin

      and that if I think it is quiet,
         then I must be the kid

with a chocolate
 smudged hand
  in the cookie jar

There is always one left

Breakfast with his high chair
       facing the orchard
where blighted peaches litter
the lawn. He's run out

of jam, and the blue balloon
       we tethered
       to the seat back
hangs limp.

It makes him sad, of course,
       that every balloon deflates,
that tomorrow, it won't
float at all.

He doesn't know we buried
       the snake under the peach tree,
won't remember the bushes
       the birds pecked clean.

He wants to take the string
       and run as if about to
lift off to the cloud haze,
       to the geese flocks

heading north ahead
       of the coming spring,
in search of cool water
and hope

that neither ends nor exists,
      where rot won't gut
      the peach roots
and there are no graves to visit.

Meanwhile, he dips his toast in milk.
      Strawberry jelly stains
      the surface, but he likes
the soggy bites, to him,
the moment immortal.

He's barely realized things don't
      disappear when out of sight,
      that the garden
might not recover, that
balloons never lived at all.

Such fantastic creatures

that dream riding smoke
columns into orbit, space
walks and hermetic domes,
peeking into new universes
through sub-atomic holes,
bending quantum existence
as they scratch their heads
over their sock drawer
before they shuffle unwashed
to a cluttered dinette and flake
dandruff into their cereal, and
read about the world cascading
down around them with mouths
pursed like crushed trumpets.

PART II

LAUNCH TRAJECTORY

Order imposes

Sometimes in afternoon deep quiet,
between wood-pecks when wind
dies, distant music, maybe from
rocking trees or changing weather,
someone with windows down and
radio volume at which melody blurs
ambience. Maybe mind imposes
substance onto absence, something

I learned late childhood nights when
nightmares left me sweating sheets.
There in the dark, a hum at some far
edge that wasn't the room's corner,
the song of slipping through cracks
and the wood rot crumbling doorframe,
In these moments, children gone,

my hands empty, I wonder: if the song
listens to us, what kind of instruments
are we? I know the sound of wasps
in the walls. How to hear their chewing
in the dark. How bits of the heart flake
off until all that beats is chamber
without wall and an empty hall
applauds the arrival of instruments.

Raising Her

Now, you're watering the backyard garden,
inspecting a mushroom, running around the big tree,

I through the window watching.
      For a moment, you disappear behind foliage,

and, when you emerge, we've experienced
just a little less of each other's lives.

I've watched you all along but miss it all again.

The day I ask for a goodnight hug and you say no,
the friend you meet whose name I never hear.

There will come a time when something bad
      will happen to you, and you will decide not to tell.

So many things we can't close fingers around,
but you leave prints every place you see fit.

The mirrors, the fridge door, the oven handle.
      A thousand layers of oil on the front knob.

In everyone's future is an empty road upon
which they are not.

Keep the window be open until then.

When it comes

She begs for snow, cries
at warm fronts, December
grass green, afternoons edging
seventy.

        Why won't we promise?
I want to wear my white
scarf, daddy, my boots.
        And I tell her *I'm sorry*
but I don't control the weather

When snow does come,
      we dress early.
      She chases bird shadows
      on the fresh pack,
      lines up a few snow balls
      on the roadside for the way back.

We stop at a fence,
        and she pokes
      at the frozen drips;
      Don't suck the icicles, sweetheart,
      they're more than water, they are what
            they've dripped through.

By midday, the snow blanket
      melts, lawns glisten like fresh cuts.
      At the window, warm, lucky,
        we watch a squirrel bound across slush,

And though I can't say it will snow again,
She tells me that *next time she'll,*
next time she'll,
next time she'll.

Tilling Grief

For weeks after they buried their child,
      the rest of the family looked
like gravediggers as they broke their garden
      in checked flannel shirts
and frayed hem jeans, leaning against shovel
      hafts, looking to each other

so little one would assume they'd not spoken in days, they lay
porous black weed blocks, beat in copper sheets
      to block the slugs,
hammer beams to wall the bed, and twist tillers to churn the clay.

Young winds ruffle their hair. Dirt under their nails, rolled cuffs,
they'll drive to town for celery and peanut butter, juice, eggs.
Wave at familiars and strangers alike. Chat up the grocery

clerk like some old Pete they've known years and laugh until
their car doors close. The world becomes their own again,
but still they become pantomime as they roll between derelict

shopping carts. Their hands too tired to hold any
      other notion of truth.
At home, they'll crook grocery bags and regard the garden
like memories that ripple fingers through their faucet thoughts.

Every seed planted, after all, a burial. Maybe it will rain, maybe
they'll hear that rain on leaves sounds different
      from rain on fresh soil,
that voices after planting are different over sprouts and in chapels,

that tears wept in rain can't be stolen by God.

That night, they'll ease
feet up besides mostly empty plates to a dead
    channel's white noise,
dream of baby cries or mice squealing in owl
    claws, roll over enough

                for crumbs to spill from their chests.

Family holiday

Mirage in charcoal smoke over fever hot grill,
fat-drip embers flare. My son watches the flame,
doesn't know how to walk near burning things
      or how skin pops on hot metal,
while my wife rustles on the couch sweating
into blankets on the third pneumonia day.

Beyond the rail, dogs fret on chains, and information
crisscrosses among satellites while our black cat
snores on the armchair and our snake snoozes
      under its false sun, the evening otherwise without stars,
over shoddy decks that fall from houses.

Nothing really keeps the whole affair upright under my feet
      other than knots and popped nails,
and my son hovers in the doorframe.
I've tried to tell him we can't trust the deck,
      that every answer about a journey's end
      is how and when, so I flip the burgers,
watch cheese melt, congeal on metal,
      gasp with smoke.

The things I need to know

I do want hope, belief
in intercession. That my children,
if in need, could expect bread.

To know them is to know the dirt
engrained lines of their shoeless feet
as they belly sprawl over coloring books.

Just one state over, a blue newborn found
in a blue cooler beneath a speed limit sign.

This, exactly, has happened before: a life
as iteration of the facets of human cruelty,
what I read the first occurrence only
to me – tragedy sealed in Ziplocs
and four-wheel drive Suburbans parked
windows up in summer sun.

Blame it on snakes or belts or lineages
of fists, but my children are too real
to allow anyone such grace.

I watch them totter about in pajamas.
They bicker about games and turns
and who looks at whom. Loud with life,
they dip crackers in milk and brush crumbs
off their lips with forearms as they dance,

make it hard to understand that as humans,
something monstrous lives in us all.
No parent can be innocent
and expect to keep their children

the same while they sing bedtime.

After mine are tucked in, I lie
in bed under the fan as the dog
circles its rug. Tomorrow, again,
I look for new roads, choose one
that leads to more than that.

Things you don't need to know

I've gotten used to it, that low ring
of the quarterly emergency siren
test for the Sequoyah Plant.
Like the horizon is a wineglass
the world runs a finger over.
I've seen the blue evacuation
signs on the roadside
but the first time I heard it,
I knelt on the living room floor
as we built the edge of a puzzle.

It was roughly 10:00 am, the empty
bowl from my daughter's snack
beside us. I didn't need to recognize
the sound to recognize the warning
in its howl from how the stillness slit
and allowed it in like an open envelope.
Outside the windows, bright, sunny,
the type of clouds a painter might add
to a sky-blue nursery wall, not weather
that warrants alarms heard for miles.

Intrinsically, every day is as good a day
for a heart attack or stroke as any,
but we'd planned to make sandwiches
and have a picnic on the back patio.
Did we need to get the bag together
with whatever snacks we could carry
and the five-gallon jug and hit the road?
For her part, she adjusted the palm

that propped her chin. Waggled her feet
at the ankles, bent into the air at the knees.

She didn't know to shudder at a wolf's
howl or that hyenas didn't actually laugh.
Wild was what you saw at zoos, disaster
that thing mommy and daddy said
was special effects. She didn't yet
see the predator that arched its spikes
over the whole of humanity.
She knew to match the pieces by looking
for the color of the edges, that the bowl
was empty, the puzzle box still mostly full.

Outside the Frame

The time you slept when your son
finished his first puzzle alone.

You're at the ready, of course.
Camera on table, a thousand plans
to keep him safe.

I like to joke that the real picture
is what the camera did not capture.

That fear I can't shake.

I sit by the tub as he splashes,
listen at the monitor when he sleeps.

With every cabinet magnetically locked
and a gate across the stairs,
I'm still a shutter snap away from
the only wrong moment it takes.

There is always aperture.
Even a 360-degree camera
has a blind spot beneath,

and then I'll be laying flowers
at the feet of an eiseled photo
and paying bills that slit the throat
of who I saw as my future.

Before I'll know it, I've not gotten out

of bed so long I've developing a sore
as I scroll through his photos

and I've named the trees
so that when I call out after
midnight, something might hear.

Epigraph

Isn't it comforting that given the Laws
of Conservation and barring premature
cessation of reality, the constituent
components of that which will kill you
exist and have existed since time began?

PART III

COST OF PASSAGE

Hidden by the Horizon

Flood waters drive fire ants to grapple
into floating knots of exoskeleton.
The bottom ones drown, while the rest
ride their bodies until flows subside,
the whole less one just a new whole.

Satere-Mare women sew bullets ants
into woven leaf gloves. Their youth
bear the stings to become adult,
the whole plus one a new whole.

My daughter in her yellow dress crouches
over ants swarming a drowned beetle.
She neither knows pain of trial
nor that one day she will.

No, she crushes dandelions, picks clover.
Loves how spring sun in the garden
Warms her shoulders. Hasn't linked
the nesting hawk's flight to
the rabbit's necessary screams.

Hedgehog

Headline says they caught
     the son of a bitch
     who violated an infant.
I refuse to acknowledge his picture,
     refuse to read his name, so
I close the laptop, open the nearest
window as if a cold breath
     can actually cleanse.

Outside, beneath the moonlight
     infested leaves,
shadow trees cross tree shadows,
hide squirrels, the bucket where
     I found the drowned rat
     and dumped its indignity
down the slope because I was
     afraid to touch it.

As if we can do something about years lost
waiting for starlight to arrive.
     As if there is such thing as justice
     once there is victim.
Cut the bark right,
     and the whole tree comes down.

Why raise fists to the impulse to retreat
     into a cave mouthed
     with sharp stakes and howl at our echoes.
Slam shut the bunker blast door. Play board games,
     charcoal sketch things we left outside.
Except that real shelter is found only in people,
     that shelter must be temporary,

everything built a coincidence of roofs.

Natural Embrace

I don't know where it broke off from or how it navigated as far as my house,
but the moss-covered log wedged sideways across the creek like a child's dam.
The water ran up and over the sides, two little waterfalls, nature letting hair down.

In the mornings, mist hung over the banks with a thickness you'd expect to part
and reveal Artemis scrubbing her arms. In the winter, the new eddy froze over.
The ice encroached the flow until the current broke edges and sent them vanishing.

To the best of my knowledge, there is no geometry to liquids, and I won't pretend
to understand Newtonian fluid physics. What I understand is that walking
one evening during a heavy snow, my boots sank almost to their mouths.

There was no wind, but accumulated clumps cascaded from overhanging boughs
with a thump like a pillow falling from a bed. Nothing in particular brought me
to the stream, to the dam, to the pale, dried reeds and the shining black rocks,

but there, against the barrier, a cat, frozen and drowned, its eyes frosted.
Perhaps it too had gone for a late-night patrol, a route that crossed the log

a hundred times. It could be a lie, but I've heard it claimed fatal hypothermia

is falling into warm sleep, that drowning is a most painful and terrifying way to die,
that one can't actually experience death because we're incapable of perceiving
the cessation of time. It's been asserted that there is only a limited window

in which matter is able to exist, that it's only a matter of time before existence
converts to energy, and that information may be eternal. I stuffed hands into pockets.
The betrayal seemed unquestionable. Tracks in the snow, soon swept away.

How we keep tending

We jingled the lock at the gates of plenty,
chains wrapped 'round the posts
patted for keys at all our pockets.

Behind us, the land of crows and locusts,
scoured fields tilled in rows of rust.
Beyond the fence slat, scattered

critters skitter among brush, nosing worm
burrows and ant hills. *There*, we whispered,
ones we still eat.

On one horizon, trees gnarl arthritic hands
and supplicate for rain. On the other,
smokestacks and scarecrows bask.

As jackals call twilight, it's time to shake
the gates. Our children turn to face the setting sun
but do not say about what they cry,

rattle cold hardeness as they blow kisses
at the moon and prayers to the sky.
They don't know to listen

to our rattling breath and greying hair,
don't know it's more than
a long walk back to the fire.

Anthill at the mailbox post

There comes a point for us all
when more people
we know have died
than still live.

You know that in a church
somewhere a crowd
plays Bingo while in another
a congregation honors
the god they keep betraying
in their hearts.

No one is ever more
than a few feet from a spider
and the combined weight
of ants on this planet
is greater than
that of human beings.
How much soil do they move
in one day?
Are we capable of the same?

You tighten your peacoat
as you walk towards
your car from work.
It's finally a cold
you feel in your fingers
as you avoid the branches
but crunch the leaves.

The strap of your satchel chafes,
and you're tired from staying up

to monitor the third day of the
second week of your son's cough.
You tell yourself you'd rather
stayed in bed than rise,
that given choice you'd tighten
the shutters and refold the curtains
against the light, well aware
you're lying to yourself, that
you won't sleep enough anyway.

There's something you can't
turn off even as you're sewing
yourself shut like a poem
in an envelope, why you keep
your bedside stocked with
melatonin, Ambien, notepad
and pen, a stripped-down app
on your phone for things
that must come out typed.

You hope maybe one day
they'll see it and understand
that everyone is a church
one must kneel inside to pray
and that you so dearly envied
the ants. How they exit and enter
their little hills. How under the ground
they meet in burrows and talk
with scents and touches of their antennae.
How they move without regret,
without sorrow for what they left behind
because their whole life built it.

The composition of the planets

My daughter lamps over her brother's shoulder
while he leafs through a book he still can't read,
and Jupiter has more in common with the
sun than the inner planets. The book
is about Pluto, but Earth from our neighbor's
vantage looks more like hydrogen.

Sitting on the couch, they look so like each other
while they share a blanket and smiles. It's not science,
you know, the composition of the planets. It's a matter
of being, of matter being its own sake. Understanding
where the carbon and water are places, ourselves
under the microscope.

Meanwhile, everything to them is science, study,
testing, the confirmation of data because they
haven't forgotten that science in practice is a
synonym for play. That on their knees in the driveway
a mound of dirt might contain all the knowledge
in the world if blown on just right.

When I grow up

He killed his ex-girlfriend with a stun gun to the head,
her tied to a chair, him high on cocaine.
As teenage neighbors, we played
wiffle ball, caught frogs in the creek.

When I was even younger, the neighbor I played
dinosaurs with secreted his father's gas can,
poured a rivulet down the alley, and watched fire
flow until he thought to burn a neighbor's house.

I'm almost relieved when I sit at sunset with my coffee
as my children chase the cats with raucous giggles.
Having hung up the phone and tabled it,
I allow myself to admit that *someone's* child

will be the one on the news in twenty years,
the one your old friends call you about because
oh my god have you heard, and I'm ashamed
to hope this lowers the odds it will be mine.

Maybe my daughter dons the toy stethoscope
to count the heartbeat of a plastic banana.
Learns what it sounds like on the inside,
swamping me in envy at the ease

with which she believes she knows the heart
of plastic fruit because it is so much harder
to read the face of innocence into the future.
When I ask what she wants to be

when she grows up, she says, *The sun.*
What if that wasn't possible? *A firetruck.*
And we laugh and laugh that already she
knows her future is something else.

The handles of axes waiting to be held

The Third Noble Truth of the Buddha doesn't know
      a thing beyond flower beauty
      and what gnaws in the body's deepest, frozen pockets
or that down the hall in the bedroom, the children's beds.
      In the beds, the children. They cuddle their stuffed
      dinosaurs who they sometimes love more
      than each other. When you ask them about
their dreams, they're uncertain what you mean
      and make up answers.

When Basho wrote haikus about splashing frogs and
      yearning for Kyoto, he did so in the context
      of his journals, laying down necessary precedents.
You tell them that one day everything living will become
      remains. That the dance of spring is one of four
      seasons but next year is a lie.
They will live beyond you, you say. A form of immortality,
      Plato claimed. Dumas's Richelieu said betrayal
      is a matter of dates; and no doubt

you've got it wrong enough to let them down, to leave them
      ill-equipped to don suits of themselves and commit
      to tending the well they draw their spirit from.
Everyone that ever lived stood a life's distance between
      themselves and the end of all times. Birth is
      a precipice on which all humans wobble.
The sheer winds come to take account, but truth is we live
      in the black until we don't, our ledger in leaf wraps
      tied with dried roots, buried.

Have I forgotten the songs

1.

Have I forgotten the songs my mother
used to sing

>   the lily petal lilts and slurs
>   lazy ticks of a tired parent
>   knelt at bed's edge
>   with too much yet to do
>   to curl up beside

that warm palm to
forehead

>   I'll never know again
>   and it leaves me
>   a little less safe
>   a little more damaged
>   crumpled in a ball
>   like a napkin

under the sheets
after things fall apart
to the coffee edges
        of daylight

2.

>   except the lilts and cadence your mother placed

in the second and third words
of the song   and the palm

she placed on your forehead;
in your memories you can't tell between
        words and pictures in voice,

tattoos of tongue etched enough times
to become truth, the way your mother's
songs became truth, the way truth

has been a lilt of voice
not the voice itself   fingerprint
dried in fresh concrete

3.

Your feet are too small for shoes
        your hand's in a finger of one of my gloves.

        They say you learn your mother's voice
                in the womb

                and she loves to sing, sing, sing.

4.

I'd lay with the sheets smoothed out
        like napkins tucked under my chin
my fingers like hanger hooks
        over a closet rod

At least a hundred black crickets
     atop the concrete under the street light
and they hop like time-lapse chess knights
     with a thousand new stories

But my mother sung me bed time songs
     every night with her hand on my forehead
teasing the front of my hair and smoothing it back
     as if to sweep bad dreams

to the back of my mind
     to the back of my bed
          to fall through the crack
               between mattress and wall

5.

Do you remember the coarse slap of freedom
     the first time you called and we did not come?

Know my mother came here from overseas
     worked since she was twelve

     because childhood was something
     one left behind like a Motherland?

     Her father's hands would sweat
          when she brought home her check.

     Told her she was lucky to keep her own buck.

One can't separate such things
    from melody
        but she crooned through it all

    through the coarse percussion of the stomp
        of her father's boots in the hall.

6.

As a little girl, my mother swallowed a kuna coin.
    It went down by millimeters and so
    afraid her mother would beat her
        she curled up in her bed
        under a blanket
    and waited to die.

As a little girl my mom drank from a wash basin
    on a scorching day and contracted typhus.

    When the fever peaked her mother wrapped
        her in her blanket and carried her
        up the mountain to the barracks

and begged the soldiers *take her to the mainland*
    to the hospital.

7.

I hope one day we will stand
    on the ocean-walk of Zadar
listen to the sea organ's whalish song
    as fisherman kick heels against the concrete dike

and cast rods for eels and snapper.
   Return to that restaurant
where we raised our glasses to shout *Zivjeli!*
   I hope you'll hear the notes
she scrawled into the sheet music
    of her heart when she'd run here barefoot
before occlusions and arterial plaque
   and mini-strokes.

8.

Twenty years later find yourself driving

back and forth by the house
   not because you'll find her
     but one might smell garlic

     in a place it's never been cooked

or place faith in wasps in the walls
   nightly clicking song of chitin and spit
   nest of thousands years in the making

Something that the universe can agree on is that
   emptiness fills   with cold fingers

and that the edges are stingers that vibrate for our palms.

I'm tired of pressing my hands to the plaster.
   No one learns the song
     so the wasps forgot to sing.

Clack of branches on glass. Rain on siding. Wind enough for
tornados.

9.

With the headphones on and the wire half out the jack
    I picked up broadcasts from who knows where.

Sometimes broken music mash ups of country and jazz
    laced with hellfire preachers
    noise you'd expect over the opening credits
        of the apocalypse.

Sometimes I'd fall asleep at the computer
        between voices unintelligible
        beyond their garbled tone.

    Among gray static threads
        sound is wire that transmits copper,

        frayed now   bundled
        and bound to tangle

My throat too knotted to inhale.

10.

Probability says that if you hit enough notes
you'll play a symphony
if you sing enough renditions
    one version will be your master craft.

The method is the trying
    the way we hold on
        to her Ellis island signature
    the way your mother holds on
        to a static filled voicemail.

We find scraps of voice like newspaper
    in the corners of our mind
        the broom bristles of time
    don't fully reach

the way you're getting ready for bed one night
    and setting a glass of water on the end table
    means you're five years old again
    and your arm just broken

and there she sits on a stool or a chair
    brushing your hair with her knuckles
        and her smile is a song
    open with singing.

11.

The next time you have dinner
    don't ask about it
        because she won't remember either.

It's not something you recite.

The fact that it is lost is what makes it
    sound like it does.

If it were recorded
        the music would be something
               that could be made.

Were that so
        then ghosts would be real
        and maybe you could hope
        that the song was too.

PART IV

PATH OF STONES

The perpetuity of hands

Trees wither
first in leaves
like people
thirst as
dried streams
claw skies
for unseen
things in
the name of belief
in the name
of their fathers
who wrapped
roots around
their throats
while they
in nakedness
sloughed curled
bark to forest bed
grew around the
garrote and wept
seeds to sleep
in rain among
things that rot
and fungus
that feeds upon
dreams
but judge
not knives
that carve
initials
inside hearts
forgive them
for falling
in love
and believing

in the perpetuity
of hands
clasped
and left prints
while rot
cancers
the phloem

Laughing Rats

Know this: it's in the walls. In the crawlspace and attic.
They say there is nowhere a rat can survive where they are not.

They laugh with both inhale and exhale when tickled, when
they wrestle and chase, one of sixty-five species known to laugh,
that know joy.
                              Delight in unlikely brightness,
swat the soap bubbles that rise from the sink,
rake the yard until the frog hops from the brush.

Let your children chase everything they can
            And never turn down a wrestling match.

Giggle between breaths because laughter puts to air
the real nature of our souls
            and because on the nights without light,
when your body
is a tightening spring,
            knees to chest,   face in hands,

dust lies thickest on the smallest beds in the house.

Yet - insulation remains, pink tufts that bed wires and pipe,
nests where the rats have stashed their stolen treasures –

a thread spool, a tic-tac box, the twisty tie from a bag of bread.

How I believe in ghosts

I won't lie – I believe in ghosts, marks left at coordinates,
haunting their cosmos moment, billions of souls strewn along
Earth's wake like a comet tail back to where the planet
was when life began. Our solar system travels 515 thousand
miles per hour, a speed we can't fathom because it's irrelevant to
our experience, and never experiences the same galactic
coordinates twice. 230 million years completes our journey
around the galactic center, a center pulled more than a million
miles per hour, every bit of it drifting outward 67 kilometers per
second. The objects headed outward at the edge of the universe
do not have destinations because there, destinations
don't exist. A wild corkscrew, our path. Most of us
will travel over 300 billion miles along the stellar plane
in our lifetime. If you are a ghost, that's how far behind
you are left. Difficult to imagine greater loneliness
as I relax beside my son and gaze at evening. Barefoot,
he pokes at garden dirt in search of something to crawl
on his palm; a snail, a pillbug, those big black ants
he loves to talk to. To him, everything has voice worth
a listen. Above, the first stars emerge, but there: a vestige
of sun caught on a cloud. I point him to it. He says
it's the ghost of light and asks if real ghosts exist.
I say, "No, not the way you mean it anyway." He nods.
Sticks his thumb into soil, brushes aside a dead grub.
"That's okay," he says. "I'll believe in them anyway."

Why you don't want the gates open

In paradise, it rains and rains
until the mud runs rivers

down the streets and sweeps
mailbox posts from driveways.

In the dark, there, you can always
hear the song of the waters

through the still curtain
and the double pane,

piccolo droplets from eaves
the bass moan of heavy flow.

Somewhere tires grip asphalt,
a siren cries for the wounds

it races towards and those
who it will leave to mourn.

The secret, of course, is that
all floods must lead to flotsam,

to the bobbing of the dead
face down in the still spots.

We couldn't be more water
and remain ourselves,

but somehow our skins
keep it out like Ziplocs.

One day, you could walk
the water's edge; if you follow

far enough, a vantage
will come eventually.

For now, squirrels on the roof.
Branches that blow free

from trunk that clatter
on shingle. You never need

to ask twice what was the sound
of a tree falling on your neighbor's

house. You just hope there won't
be a splintered crib, that you'll

look away fast enough not to know.

The small current

Sun doesn't mean to warm us as the rock under the trickle
doesn't mean to cut our heels as currents can't help eroding
their banks. One of my high school best friends hung himself
in the half-flight stairwell with his belt just off a room full of ash
and cat shit and chest high stacks of takeout boxes. No doubt
there were amber plastic bottle and those round white lids.

The water finds its way down no matter how subtle the slope
or how eddies distract the flow with their frothy swirls until
a lowest point pool where the surface spreads in search of outlets
to dribble through. If there is exit, it will be found, so I stop too,
dip fingers among clustered amphibian eggs clinging to cattail
leaves fallen to rot as crayfish dart for crevices and minnows
dash at what specks waft from the folds of my knuckles.

.

Read the leaves

We can't help crunching them
even if we try not to move

Tumble of things meant to glide
broken bits in slow cascade
trying to forget gravity

trying to become basin
and that which fills

falling drops
elongate because days shorten
and acorns clatter the roof

Herald Nature shakes
Her bag of bones
bares teeth amid branches
thorn naked trunks

the forest floor
strewn with Her clothes

the wind will dance incoming
moonlight serenades in choir with
an ecstasy of coyotes

and here we stand as gaunt coop hens
behind glass air and press palms against
growling dream futures

where we don't hide our seeds
and turn on lights before sunset
because we're at peace with the dark

Updraft

let's write ourselves like air
        inside paper lanterns
        that we let drift
    into the sky
      the sea
      our veins

the elements
     will blur the ink until
     we can only hope
       they can be read
     by the god
     of our choice

short of that
     the devils we love

until then
     we sing the wind
     that splinters our hope
     at the trunk

The last human apology

I.

I presume it will be made in a desert of our making,
because we never learned   the lesson of Venus,
because we believe   in intervention
        and a litany of miracles,
because I am an optimist, because I believe
        in the resilience of the human spirit,
because I believe in spite

II.

Persevere through intolerable conditions. Claw across rocks.
Leave behind flesh in shreds in intolerance. Sometimes, we are so
small many of us can't find ourselves until we step on our own
bones.

Many will abandon their children because parched throats make
the hardest sobs,   and some will carry them on their backs
                no matter how deep the stones gash.

III.

Deserts embody the memory of rain,
and no one is human after their mother is dead.
I pray it is made by no one I know, met, dreamt.
There is one in every life, the final one heard before.
If there is a first, there is a last by definition, and we either

make them or owe. I'm sorry to both my children from the start,
because I started failing them before they were born.
Maybe before I was.

IV.

Maybe it will be made by a being on Mars who looks back to the
once blue dot
       from where its ancestors came and wonders how they
managed
         to send themselves so far and how shameful it is
            to bear this new original sin.

Children, hear me out: no doubt I will fear I spent my time wrong,
that every day worked slipped another dollar from the wallet of
our time,
and before the end I will be calling the bank again and again
        about all those zero balances.

Maybe one late evening will come, a fire, embers grown low
before
       a dirty young man who gave up on roofs when mother died
in a sleeping bag
       lies in her sleeping bag and runs thirsty fingers into soil,

lies that *he wishes things were different, that he could*
give it all back, that there was water until there wasn't
and thinks his words are a rambling brook of will imposed on air,
unaware that even asking forgiveness violates the still sanctity.

V.

Won't be to maples or elms, raspberry brambles or palms,
          and old trees hung with Spanish moss.
Won't be to those orcas with brutalist marbling, skimming
pike in silt, or rainbow trout among river rocks. No doubt these
will all be long dead in our wake, buried with bees, butterflies,
peppered moths and garden snails. It won't be meant.
Without a future, convictions are obsolete. When the past
becomes heat mirage on the highway, it's either falsity
or nothing for our boot heels to wear down approaching.
Before we get there, we will be barefoot on asphalt wondering
if those gnarled things at the end are what we once called toes.
          There is no simple way to tell you: I am not who you think
I am.
You'll know this better in time. When the myths dispel. When you
see
the world I helped build despite my best intentions. Perhaps one
day
you'll drive back by our garden boxes and find the frames
persist beyond the long-withered crops.

The Sickly Tree

yellow spotted sickness
    tell the heart

which part
    is safe to eat

PART V

THE NINTH FILTER

Parenting

In the bedroom, my daughter sleeps.
The hard truth is life will likely
not take her as far as I'd like
and one day she will weep
in ways too hard to imagine.
When she wakes, I will feed her
frozen waffles for breakfast
because I can't offer anything better,
and then I'll kneel on the kitchen floor
and roll one of her balls towards the living room.
She will run after, her gait carefree but unsure.
As she crouches to grasp it in both hands
and raises it in victory,
I will triumph with her,
forget to wonder
who will bury whom.

Fighting Fermi

1.

If there is hope, it lies
      more distant
      than we can comprehend

until we've proven more than grounds
      washing up against
      Fermi's Ninth Great Filter.

Our best chance is that fate makes us
      the bedbugs of the universe, that our Mother
      gave is more than the imagined jingle of keys.

In a place where sound cannot exist,
      neither does silence.

      Fermi's door lacks locks, hinges or frame,
         keeps nothing out, nothing in,
         promises to threaten us with futures.

2.

What else do I say at the bedside
of those about to pass? To keep them
from wondering if they'll be the first
to die on that set of sheets?

A parent, grandparent, a beloved teacher,

nose gone purple as their toes,
nurses hover in the background.

Can I tell them the world isn't less
worn than before they were born,
that at best they forestalled collapse
by milliseconds?

3.

I'm here, I
want to say,
but the want
makes me feel
like an intruder,
like I don't
deserve a voice
around your death.

4.

Thankfully, this poem is not about the cosmos but of holding your
hand.
Of knowing silence can be a thousand answers, of knowing there
is
soon to be only one answer to every question I ask. The story of
every passing tells of strength to press on, story itself proof it did.
We must remember that at the real end, things are never alright
and never were, but that is not the reason stories end: we tire
of the telling, of waiting for the doctors to come nonetheless.

5.

Earlier, an elderly man walked with toddler steps
to the vending machine and stood dollar in hand five minutes
before he leaned his forehead against the plastic front.

Everyone needs a friend when the moon is not enough.

Loose threads hung from the pockets of his slacks,
his swollen ankles bulging over shoes too tight.
The veins over the bone looked angry.

6.

Hard not to hunger
    when I haven't
        changed socks in days.
When my shirt bears
    all manner of
        unidentifiable smudges.
When I think
    no one should be
        allowed to die
without knowingly
    feeling wind on skin
        for the last time.
When human genome maps
    yield nothing
        about the heart.
When satellites show
    every corner of the globe
        without revealing

what to say
     to the man so distressed
          he can't decide between
          pretzels and chips.

7.

These glass moments are when I'm astonished
we reached the moon and doubt we'll get farther.
It's not for lack of faith. Beta fish in shelved jars
have faith in the water, in the oxygen in the water,
in the little plastic plant that competes for space.
Perhaps all species live in such solar systems
under the lids of interstellar medium, nothing
farther than the fish in the next jar, the man
in the next room over when you want to speak
dying words and you can't see any ears.

8.

In the corner of your own room,
mounted up by the ceiling, a muted TV.
A badly imagined grainy transmission.

In the night level lights of the room,
both of us looked up like a child might
as they pray. They haven't yet earned

the need for humility before God, haven't
yet learned the meaning that underlies
the words for the things they will one day

do wrong.

9.

Distance is meaningless if the end goal is eyesight
and a heartbeat.

This is the time when the soul's best interest lies
in undoing object permanence.
>   To forget the stars
>   were the second thing
>   we thought would never leave.

>   For the world to be flitting lights
passing behind folding screens and hung curtains.

>   Or else the EKG stenographs
>   the only life story we've got left,

even as the smell of antiseptic becomes the smell
of butterflies in the dark.
>   Hands never stop holding
even once they are no longer being held.

An exhale is an unwanted gift to the world.
>   Few things are more intimate
>   than cleaning someone else's fingers.

Grasping branches in the current

It would be irresponsible not to hold on. The water rush,
over rocks, water parting around granite distinct from water
parted by branch, by human limb. A million differences
to account for, to name, list in sand swept away by wind
and feet that follow: the place where you took your first step,
your first word sounded like this: the way I held you the first
time you cried someone's hurt in my arms. If holding all this
in such a sorry vessel bucking the turbulence allowed sanctuary
in our heart's rock pool, maybe then, we could become intent
on movement, the flex of elbow and knee, silent churn
of lung sac against rib. On how our insides don't scrape
holes in all our soft parts so well that we proceed
as if they can't.
                              Otherwise, I might ask the fox
on the shore, the red wolf, the possum burrowed
at the rock's base, where the water goes if they're not
too busy with hind paws kicking dirt over something
dead to wonder how the flow finds roots through stone
pores, the slivers where edges meet and cease being edges,
but once you start to navigate by the stars all paths
become lines between points in expanse. The truth is
you know the smaller hearts will one day exceed your own.
Everything is mended once it turns to dirt. Soon, moss
invades and leaves it soft under bare feet on stream bottom,
shifting like the whole bed is alive until the day
the moon breathes frost upon water trapped inside
fissures and winter freezes burst them open like melons.

Yesterday, the split of prokaryotes

My daughter props palms on the counter and surveys the cutting board
like a queen over a world map. The Isle of Mushroom. Parsley Peninsula.
Garlic, Parmesan steer the ship. She can read the recipe,
but she wants me to guide her.
                     Up until recently,
she spoke of all past events as yesterday. The past
is soup, each new marjoram memory, an herb pinch, a carrot sliver,
shaved white onion. I would correct her, tell her what happened a year ago,
or last month. She slipped often, but now she's replaced 'yesterday'
with "remember when I was two."
                 Part of me likes to think
that something in her, in all of us, travels at the speed of light,
careens through the stars like something fired from a pulsar,
blurs the boundaries of our universe like the windowpane test,
like her smile through cheese cloth, like the hot spring of boiling
broth and steeping stock leaching something that lived in the bones.
                When it's done
we can all be ladled into jars because our minds are too slow
to keep up but damn it smells so good in the kitchen and I don't remember when I was two
                    or remember that tomorrow
we will visit the pond I grew behind yesterday, beat our way through
the skunk cabbage and sit among south shore cattails to observe

what state the tadpoles are in. Obviously, dinner is not done,
but at her age 'stir for three minutes' is like terminal diagnostics.
The onions in their butter haven't yet caramelized, and I've yet
to toss in the rest of the aromatics.

        Time, blind and gnawing

at quantum foam, writhes its nose into pores wide enough to allow
in indefinite middleness; the sunrise, the horizon flares that
rainbow
minutes of mist and dew and cast the longest shadows. Her hands
flat in the flour. Her prints on her apron, all over the counter,
the cabinet handles. A little puddle in a dirty bowl in the sink
in which paramecium waft their flagellum and know nothing of
what
small a sliver of the whole stew is their universe. I don't
remember,
but when I was two must be handprints in flour.

        Spilled sugar sparkles.

Soul Brawl

You're not dead yet,
so there's that.
Though the day's
not done
and it's just bare
bones and bare feet
in the soil
under leaf-stripped
branches
in the soul,

every fight waged
in hospital beds
digs deeper
than bare knuckle
and white sheets
checked in that hotel
where doors
sleep in empty rooms
unlocked
and always lit,

and you know they're
talking about you,
those machines
with lights
and numbers
and scribbling
needles, bellows
that pump sighs
and IVs that drip
life in cubic millimeters,

but you're fading by
inches and no one's
ever agreed on a
unit of measurement
for the length
of a moment collapsing
into a white speck
caught in a trunk
creaking breeze.

In the sky
over I75 south,
A meteor falls.
It's more than
a shooting star,
a white streak
so fast I'm done
seeing it before
I know I saw it.

Somewhere
on a hillside,
it lodges.
Somewhere
the grass burns.
Wherever
that is,
A tree nearby
with cracked
bark all over.

There, that is
the place where
there is heat,

nacent, burgeoning.
A flicker
in the dark
among the grasses
and brush,
Soon smoke,
fire, then ash.

Scrying

My wife tells me in the lamplight
after everyone else has gone to sleep
that sometimes she hopes

our children won't have children
because they will suffer what
we leave behind, that we are

the last lucky ones to whom plenty
means more than we need
rather than more than we have.

I can't comprehend how my hypothetical
grandchildren might live. They'll use
food science as one word. Land

on asteroids, Mars, control computers
with their minds. Maybe they'll
pre-program their dreams like mixed tapes.

My daughter and I talk about this
and that; her classes, my day, the movie
we watch, but could we evolve beyond

mouths and simply think with each other?
Can we still have hands that can hold?
My wife and I lie on the couch, tired,

the sound low. Outside, trees on the slopes,
millions of cicadas and crickets in them,

the darkness shattered infinitely in their song.

Retrograde

Galaxies expand apart at a rate that leaves no hope of crossing
        even if we devise teleportation
                the distance   we will never comprehend

heat transfer needs contact so let me hold
        the days where I make every excuse to sidle up
        to my kids on the couch
                watch them discover bugs   in the garden

        They grow further by days
                the best things ever look   they look in memory
                or when they're about to be

give me chance to consider how parts should move
        how black holes might vent into other universes
        where maybe we tend the world well,

        maybe, there, gravity repels
        starshine   time circles back   and comets chase

their own flaming tails like our dog before a storm. We've sought
wormholes,
        and the best deal we got is our dreams
                in the contract of the universe,
        a return policy   a warranty   90 billion years

        and either resurrection or a subscription cycle

Meanwhile, laid bare, fallen, seeds wait
        And we'll pick them up best we can
      With our fingers in the garden digging for a future

among phosphates, sulfur, zinc, and copper.

A red wasp walks a fallen fence post   in search of
cellulose.
                    A length of old wire. Pillbugs
                    who carry whole broods
        in egg pouches   on their undersides
                    ready to burst their big bang.

The Ladybug

It's hard to drink
the poisons
despite how often
they brim and bubble
at our lips

the world is
designed to turn
our heads sideways
and our ankles
around
and make us
the moths to every
unimportant
light

which is why
I fight so hard
to watch my son
sitting on a branch
fretting around
ladybug in January
that isn't
actually there

When the path forks ahead

If it doesn't now, in the multiverse,
    your neighborhood burns
        from draught.
        Flies crawl
        inside the glass.

A cold hand on your
    neck, an empty crib
    in a room
    you leave locked.

There is silence in which your heart
    races and silence
    where it sits
    dead as a sandbag.

Find out how much silence one room can hold.
    Measure how that volume increases in proportion
    to the size of the family.

Thus, I say, take hold.
        A brass doorknob.
        A chair arm.
        The window frame.

    It is,
        there.
            Real.

            Our rarity listed

in the catalog
of quantum places.

Let's buy tickets.

The wait is long, but
the show rewards.

About the Author

Andrew Najberg is the author of *The Goats Have Taken Over the Barracks* (Finishing Line Press 2021) and *Easy to Lose* (Finishing Line Press 2008). His individual works of poetry and prose have appeared in *North American Review, Nashville Review, Another Chicago Magazine, Stoneboat Literary Journal, Louisville Review, Istanbul Review, Fleas on the Dog, Yemassee, Artful Dodge, Bat City Review, Bangalore Review, HASH Journal*, and many other journals and anthologies. He teaches at the University of Tennessee Chattanooga where he also assists with the Meacham Writers Workshop.

Thank you

Amber Najberg, Tiffany Najberg Mom, Dad, Gillian, Elliott, Richard Jackson, Kathleen Driskell, Katy Yocom, Earl Braggs, Marilyn Kallet, Art Smith, Mike Jaynes, Curt Allday, Matt Urmy, Christian Collier, Jeff Hardin, Jesse Graves, Kristi Maxwell, Molly Peacock, Lennie Hays, JoAnn LoVerder-Dropp, Elissa Petrucelli, John Anticev, Autumn Watts, Caleb Jordan, John Compton, and Nissim Lebovits, Rachel King, Ali Kominsky.